CONSCIOUS PRAISE

30-Day Devotional and Journal

JULIA IBOK ESSIEN

BALBOA.PRESS
A DIVISION OF HAY HOUSE

Balboa Press books may be ordered through booksellers or by contacting:

Balboa Press
A Division of Hay House
1663 Liberty Drive
Bloomington, IN 47403
www.balboapress.com
844-682-1282

* Scripture quotations marked NKJV are taken from the New King James Version. Copyright © 1982 by Thomas Nelson, Inc. Used by permission. All rights reserved.

** Scripture quotations marked NIV are taken from the Holy Bible, New International Version®. NIV®. Copyright © 1973, 1978, 1984 by International Bible Society. Used by permission of Zondervan. All rights reserved. [Biblica]

***Scripture quotations marked TLB are taken from The Living Bible. Copyright © 1971. Used by permission of Tyndale House Publishers, Inc., Carol Stream, Illinois 60188. All rights reserved.

Print information available on the last page.

ISBN: 978-1-9822-6957-9 (sc)
ISBN: 978-1-9822-6956-2 (hc)
ISBN: 978-1-9822-6955-5 (e)

Balboa Press rev. date: 06/23/2021

CONTENTS

GUIDE TO USING THIS PRAISE DEVOTIONAL & JOURNAL

- I encourage you to use this devotional first thing in the morning when you wake up.
- You will need a copy of the Bible, so I encourage you to get one, if you do not have already. This will allow you to read the scriptures for yourself. If you prefer an electronic version, BibleGateway.com, BibleHub.com, and the YouVersion Bible App are all easy to use.
- Most quotations included are from the New King James Version but feel free to use the Bible that you prefer. Occasionally you will see scriptures taken from other versions of the Bible such as the New International Version (NIV) and The Living Bible (TLB).
- Have your pen ready, so that you can write down your thoughts and fill out the journal section.
- Write the date as you start each new day. This will ensure that you are intentional about what you are doing. Remember to document your achievements too!
- If you miss any day, please carry on from where you stopped.

God's promise to you:

Isaiah 61:3

To console those who mourn in Zion, to give them beauty for ashes, the oil of joy for mourning, the garment of praise for the spirit of heaviness; that they may be called trees of righteousness, the planting of the LORD, that He may be glorified.

ACKNOWLEDGEMENTS

I would like to thank God for giving me the instruction and inspiration to write this book. It took patience, determination, and relying on the Holy Spirit to complete this work.

I am indebted to my husband, family, friends, and the pastors who supported and encouraged me in so many ways.

To my editors, thank you for your dedication and immeasurable support.

God bless you all.

INTRODUCTION

Today, right here, right now, you may be asking, "Why should I be thankful when all 'hell' is breaking loose, and I feel defeated?!"

This is because you find yourself at a crossroads where you feel like there is no way that any of your dreams or ambitions will come to pass.

However, I invite you to journey out of that place of gloom, where you are focused on what makes you so unhappy and, instead, look at the brighter side of life with this Praise devotional.

This is a place where you can build your trust on the one who knows everything about you and is watching over you.

I invite you on a 30-day walk, where you will learn how to create a new praise culture as you read this journal. Yes, we will spend the next month changing our countenance, uplifting our spirits, praising God! So, I say welcome and thank you.

Psalm 150:6 "Let everything that has breath praise the Lord."

This book will help you reflect on the good things that have happened in your life and praise God for sustaining you through all the challenges that came with them. So, I warn you to keep your dancing shoes close, because, as we reflect and praise God, you'll begin to dance!

I congratulate you for fighting hard and fighting well through the challenges of life. Maybe the fall was so great that you never believed you would get up, but God has kept you; and trust God, you are rising. Proverbs 24:16 "For a righteous man may fall seven times and rise again, but the wicked shall fall by calamity."

God is super proud of you, and guess what? Someone close to you has learned something from you having done it the hard way, and still persevering.

You did it and you made it! His Grace sustained you.

I hope that this book blesses and inspires you to keep pushing.

Like David, you can say, "Bless the Lord, O my soul, and forget not all His benefits!" (Psalm 103:2).

Yes, this is indeed your testimony.

That through Darkness you are going into the Light with your Conscious Praise!

Welcome to your 30 Days of Praise!

PRAISE

Conscious Praise will lead you through the Darkness into the Light.

This book invites you to praise God for the next 30 days and detail your praise journey with me.

Yes, it doubles as a devotional and journal which you can use at any point; however, I would like to encourage you to use this consistently for the next 30 days.

Say this with me: "Dear Lord, help me as I partake in this praise experience, to encounter your glory afresh in my life."

I believe that, as you use this book, you will be encouraged to praise God.

Who should praise God?

The Scripture says, in Psalm 150:6, "Let everything that has breath praise the LORD."

I believe that this means that we all, as much as we are living, should praise God.

I believe that even though you may have had some gloomy days, better days are ahead, so praise God for them. Only the living are hopeful, therefore you should praise God!

Reasons for praising God

Someone might ask, "Why are you praising God when everything around you looks incomplete?"

You may not have any good response immediately for the person because you are also thinking the same. But you see, I would have you understand that one reason for which you should praise God is "for in perfect faithfulness He has done wonderful things, things planned long ago" (Isaiah 25:1, NIV), therefore since God already planned it long ago, you don't need to worry about Him completing it.

Let me reassure you that "the Lord will perfect that which concerns you" (Psalm 138:8).

Caution

Be mindful that you can't let any situation, thought, or feeling stop you from praising God.

As you set out to participate in this praise experience, the enemy will try to stop you. He will paint pictures that create doubt, making you feel that your life has no value, and that nothing good can come to you. He will give you reasons that will make you wonder if you should bother praising God.

The Bible gives us great examples of believers who praised God in dire times. For example, in Acts 16:23, Paul and Silas were thrown into prison and while there, they prayed and sang praises to God, and the prison gates opened. Hallelujah!

I assure you that as you learn and build the habit of actually praising God, you will testify! God will open the prison doors in your life. In Jesus' name, amen!

Do not let your situation stop you from praising God. We don't read that they were embarrassed that God did not prevent them from being thrown into prison, instead, they praised God in spite of their situation.

As long as your salvation is assured, I believe that your victory cannot be denied. In Jesus' name, amen!

Sometimes, life hits us so hard that we feel like disappearing, hiding, and becoming invisible. These are all gimmicks from the enemy. What he does is paint pictures that are not real. Praise will help you to refocus your mind and attention to the true God who can do "exceedingly abundantly above all that we ask or think, according to the power that works in us" (Ephesians 3:20).

At such times, you feel defeated. You feel like you have let down your family, friends, God, and even yourself. May I encourage you today to believe that praise can help you to establish a new perspective on life. And no, it doesn't matter how hard or tough life has been, the name of our faithful God is worthy to be constantly praised. So get up and let's praise Him together.

I see you on a high pedestal of success, ignited with faith in God through praise and believing again. Praise God!

Do not confuse your experiences for your identity.

You must not listen to the adversary. The Bible says he goes around like a roaring lion seeking whom to devour. This means that as he goes around, he comes to you with pictures, lies, and make-believe events to try to distract you from trusting God with your praise.

Just like Jesus, respond with the word of God. Praise is affirming with God about who He is. You can only do that through whom He has said He is in the Bible which is His word. So, this is an experience where you will be reminding yourself of who God is and the person He has made you, in Him.

You are God's own, made in His image to succeed and prosper in life, so refuse to focus on your under-achievements; instead, focus on the glory of the future as you praise God!

One thing we must bear in mind on this journey is that praise satisfies God and brings down His glory. The Word says that "He is a rewarder of those who diligently seek Him" (Hebrews 11:6).

When you praise God, you seek him, and the Bible says "seek, and you will find" (Matthew 7:7-8). You are saying, "away with the worry." Hallelujah!

Do you know what God's presence in your life does? His presence sanctifies, makes new, and is rewarding.

So, if you sometimes feel like a failure or think that all the plans you had for yourself have failed, let me remind you of something that can uplift you. The Scripture says that in "all these things we are more than conquerors through Him who loved us" (Romans 8:37). So, even though you have been through the hardships, cried uncontrollably about your experiences, and questioned your existence, I tell you, you still have reasons to give God praise, for I see His glory revealed in your life and situation. Your testimony will be like that of the man who received his sight in John 9:1-12.

As you come on this praise journey with me, I invite you to sit still and encounter His warm presence. Like David, I pray that God will reveal Himself to you as a shepherd that you can trust to take care of your needs, so you need not worry.

DAY 1:

Praise God for His Blessings

Psalm 68:19

Blessed be the Lord,
* Who daily loads us with benefits,*
* The God of our salvation! Selah.*

Caroline sat looking out from her window and reminiscing over the last 20 years. It was a quiet night, and she could remember all that had happened, like it was yesterday. As she stared outside, looking at the lights and reflections from the other apartments, she heard a knock on her door; it was a stranger who was lost and needed some direction.

He mentioned that he had been travelling for some days and desperately needed to get to his final destination so he could rest.

After giving him directions, Caroline shut her door, thinking that her life was like that of the stranger who had been on a journey and desperately wanted to get to his destination.

She had sometimes thought that she was so close, but then realized it was still some time to get there, and she was running out of physical strength.

Thankfully, someone had recently preached to her about Jesus; how He could help her, and she had accepted Jesus as her savior. Now she was thankful that she felt renewed daily by studying His Word.

She was determined to see what trusting in God would help her to achieve in life.

Today, you too should come into God's presence with joy and thanksgiving in your heart.

Do not dwell on those things that have caused you pain in the past or any negative thing that is happening now.

Bring to mind something that has made you happy or hopeful.

What has God helped you to achieve in your past? Think of what He has helped you accomplish in your life.

Count your blessings and praise God for doing all the fantastic things that He has done in your life.

He is God, and none can compete with His existence, supremacy or power. He speaks of Himself and asks a question in Jeremiah 32:27: "I am the Lord, the God of all flesh. Is anything too hard for Me?"

I wish I could hear you say, "absolutely nothing."

You're right; there is absolutely nothing too complicated for the Lord to handle. Therefore, as you praise Him for His blessings today, you are putting a delivery stamp on the requests you have made according to His will. "If you ask anything in My name, I will do it" (John 14:14).

You have been wonderfully made, precious in his sight; look around you and now give him praise.

It is our first day of praise, so let's praise God for His goodness in our lives.

AFFIRMATION

Today, I bless the Lord for His goodness in my life. I turn on the shower of blessings, and I leave this running because the Word says my cup is running over; therefore, this water shall never stop running. It is overflowing, increasing, and the blessings are noticeable. Hallelujah!

JOURNAL

List one thing that you are most grateful for today.

Day 1

DAY 2:

Praise God for the Days Ahead

Psalm 147:7

Sing to the Lord with thanksgiving;
  Sing praises on the harp to our God.

Peter was looking at his payslip; things had been so slow the last year. He had plans to become a medical doctor, but one thing had led to another, and with failures, disappointments, and anguish, Peter could barely survive each day.

He relied on friends and family to help him live one day at a time. Peter decided that it was time to praise God for the days ahead.

He saw an ad for a small company looking to recruit an assistant, so Peter applied for the position and was hired. On his first day, he was excited to meet new people and learn more about his role and tasks.

Not long after he started, Peter realized that he was experiencing challenges on the job and he considered quitting.

A day in a Christian's life may look like a day in the life of an organization's new employee. Like Peter, they get excited with anticipation at joining this reputable firm after rigorous interviews. However, not long after, they begin to experience various challenges that sometimes tempts them to quit.

5

Peter didn't quit, he stayed on, and years later he became a manager in this organization.

Today, I want to encourage you to stay on and give God praise for helping you go through every challenge. Praise Him, for the days ahead are beautiful.

Like David in Psalm 42:11, say to yourself, "Why are you cast down, O my soul? And why are you disquieted within me? Hope in God; for I shall yet praise Him, the help of my countenance and my God."

Yes, say these words to yourself and be determined to praise God, notwithstanding the hardship you experience.

You have been promised a good life by your heavenly Father, and He does not go back on His word.

Therefore, today be thankful for the days ahead.

AFFIRMATION

Thank you, God, for the days ahead. When I go through deep waters and great trouble, you will be with me. When I go through rivers of difficulty, I will not drown. When I walk through the fire of oppression, I will not be burned up; the flames will not consume me (Isaiah 43:2, TLB). Thank you, Jesus!

JOURNAL

List at least two things that you are thankful for, or write a lesson to yourself about staying in the present and enjoying the journey.

Day 2

DAY 3:

Praise God for the Harvest

Psalm 107:21-22

Oh, that men would give thanks to the LORD for His goodness,
And for His wonderful works for the children of men!

Let them sacrifice the sacrifices of thanksgiving,
And declare His works with rejoicing.

Justina felt terribly bad about how disdainfully she had been treated by her boss at work, and she planned to start producing low quality work. She conspired with other employees and they decided to siphon off the client's funds and materials belonging to the company.

This would be an ungodly way to act, and Justina being a Christian, knew that she should not do or repay evil, as we are instructed in Romans 12:17-19: "Repay no one evil for evil. Have regard for good things in the sight of all men. If it is possible, as much as depends on you, live peaceably with all men. Beloved, do not avenge yourselves, but rather give place to wrath, for it is written, 'Vengeance is Mine; I will repay,' says the Lord."

Apart from this, we are taught in Genesis 8:22, that seedtime and harvest will not cease. Therefore, as long as we plant good seeds in our businesses, and/or career, the harvest will definitely come.

Today, thank God for the harvest that is coming to you. Hallelujah!

A farmer who plants seeds patiently expects that the crops will germinate and grow; so, like that farmer, step into today with an expectation that your seeds will grow.

Maybe you have planted seeds but have not seen any growth yet; be encouraged and know that some seeds take time to grow. What is important is that you are planting, so keep planting good seeds.

Plant your seeds in your family, marriage, career, and education, and trust that they will grow. Just be intentional about planting good seeds always.

I can assure you that God will give you the increase, "for the scriptures cannot be broken."

The Word of God, which is a seed that has been planted in your heart, will grow, and you will reap a good harvest.

AFFIRMATION

Dear God, thank You for reminding me that there is always a harvest. Teach and help me to plant good seeds in my family, marriage, career, and education, and I trust that they will grow. I am intentional and plant good seeds always. I trust that You will provide a bountiful harvest.

JOURNAL

Take stock of what seeds you have been planting lately.

Write down the things that you need to work on in your life.

Decide to plant good seeds today and expect your harvest.

Day 3

DAY 4:

Praise God for the Ability to Choose

Psalm 118:1

Oh, give thanks to the LORD, for He is good!
For His mercy endures forever.

Welcome to Day 4 of Praise!

I hope that you woke up ready to praise God for his goodness in your life.

Today, let's praise God for the ability to choose. God does not force Himself on us, instead He gives us the freedom to invite Him into our lives.

Linda walked into the store and indicated that she liked an item. While she was still deciding if she actually needed the item the salesgirl, who had a target to hit, mounted pressure on her to make the purchase.

Most of us, if not all, have had an experience where we felt forced to buy something.

Right now, maybe you feel that you have been badly influenced in life by certain circumstances or people; I want you to know that you have the right of choice and you can begin to thank God for the ability to choose today. Yes, right now, you are choosing to thank

God; thank Him for His wisdom that guides you and helps you to make the right decisions.

On the other hand, if you have a habit that you know is inconsistent with the Word of God but have found it hard to change or stop, I would like to remind you that your mistake(s) of the past can be forgiven if you choose to come to Christ and ask Him to forgive you. 2 Corinthians 5:17 says, "Therefore, if anyone is in Christ, he is a new creation; old things have passed away; behold, all things have become new."

You have entered a place of newness, and you can choose to live and adopt new habits. Newness should not just be in one area of your life. It should be experienced in every area. The Scripture says that if you remain in God, and his words abide in you, you will ask God anything, and it will be done for you (John 15:7).

If you ask God for the wisdom to choose right, live right, and totally submit to Him, He will hear you today. The Scripture says, "If any of you lacks wisdom, let him ask of God, who gives to all liberally and without reproach, and it will be given to him" (James 1:5).

God has given us the ability to choose to serve Him and to live right for Him. The Scripture says that he stands at the door of our heart and knocks and will only come in when we open. "Behold, I stand at the door and knock. If anyone hears My voice and opens the door, I will come in to him and dine with him, and he with Me" (Revelations 3:20).

This is awesome! God, the maker of the universe, gives us the right to choose to open the door to Him. He wants to help us get rid of the habits that are wrong in our lives; He is there to provide you and I with the wisdom to make the best choice.

AFFIRMATION

Dear God, thank you for giving me the right to choose. Today, I ask for your wisdom to guide me in all my life affairs in Jesus' name. Amen.

JOURNAL

Now that you know you can choose, what are you going to change in your life? Write down a statement describing your choice.

Day 4

DAY 5:

Praise God for a Surprise Coming to You

Daniel 2:23

I thank You and praise You,
O God of my fathers;
You have given me wisdom and might,
And have now made known to me what we asked of You,
For You have made known to us the king's demand.

Ephesians 3:20-21

Now to Him who is able to do exceeding abundantly above all that we
ask or think, according to the power that works in us, to Him be glory...

Henry already had a job and was not searching for one when his phone rang on this particular day. He picked it up swiftly, as he always did, and found that it was a recruiter at the other end of the line.

The outcome of that call was that Henry had been headhunted by a multinational company. Henry and his family celebrated this great news with some friends.

Today, I want you to put yourself in Henry's place and envision something new which is worth celebrating that is coming to you. You see, God is full of surprises for us.

The scripture says in Psalm 68:19, "Blessed be the LORD, who daily loads us with benefits."

Today, I want you to remember that God promises you His blessings every day, so praise Him for the benefits that are coming to you today. Again, He chooses to break boundaries, principles, laws, and protocols to bless His children. This is because He wants to bring His purposes to pass, and especially make the world a better place. So, expect to receive a surprise from Him today!

Can you imagine how Mary felt when the angel appeared to her and told her that she would get pregnant by the Holy Spirit and give birth to a child? This was an absolute surprise; it had never happened before!

Luke 1:26-29

"...The angel Gabriel was sent by God to a city of Galilee named Nazareth, to a virgin betrothed to a man whose name was Joseph, of the house of David. The virgin's name was Mary. And having come in, the angel said to her, 'Rejoice, highly favored one, the Lord is with you; blessed are you among women!' But when she saw him, she was troubled at his saying, and considered what manner of greeting this was."

God wants to bless and increase you; if there is anything that you have been waiting for, I want to encourage you to trust in God and believe that He is who He says He is, and that there is nothing that God cannot do. Today, rejoice in God, for he is bringing you a beautiful surprise! Hallelujah!

AFFIRMATION

Dear God, thank You for fulfilling the prophecy in my life and for Your pleasant surprises. My heart is open to receive from you today. As I walk in the counsel of the godly, may I be that person that is like a tree planted by streams of water, which yields its fruit in its season and whose leaf does not wither... whatever I do prospers (Psalm 1:3).

You have given me all things that pertain to life and godliness; therefore, today, I proclaim that You have made me glad, and I am so happy that a pleasant surprise is coming my way. Hallelujah!

JOURNAL

What is the one thing that would make you so happy if God surprised you with it?

Day 5

DAY 6:

Praise God for His Strength
to Endure Tough Times

Habakkuk 3:17-19

Though the fig tree may not blossom,
Nor fruit be on the vines;
Though the labor of the olive may fail,
And the fields yield no food;
Though the flock may be cut off from the fold,
And there be no herd in the stalls —

Yet I will rejoice in the LORD,
I will joy in the God of my salvation.

The LORD God is my strength;
He will make my feet like deer's feet,
And He will make me walk on my high hills.

I am so excited to be on this praise journey with you, and I am glad that nothing has hindered you from continuing. You are an overcomer, always.

Alice was a runner, but she was injured and almost gave up during her last competition. She could feel her muscles tightening and tearing every step of the way, but she endured and pressed on, asking God to help her until she could pass on the baton to the next person. Due to her persistence and trust that God would see her through, her team was not disqualified, but continued on and won. They remained indebted to Alice but she remained indebted to the Holy Spirit who reminded her of the scripture that says, "but those who wait on the LORD shall renew their strength; they shall mount up with wings like eagles, they shall run and not be weary, they shall walk and not faint" (Isaiah 40:31).

Today, we are praising God and trusting Him that His strength for you endures, and you will win even through the tough times in life. Yes, there are tough times that can even challenge your faith, but that is not when to give up; for when you are weak, then God can make you strong as you hold on to Him.

Like Shadrach, Meshach and Abednego held on to God for their deliverance, I pray that you receive the strength to face any challenge and stay faithful and true to God.

There are tough times that are like a drought. Times when you feel that things should be happening; when you expect the showers of blessings, but you don't even perceive mercy drops. Times when nothing seems to be happening for you. You may even be experiencing that now. I encourage you to read our opening verse again and truly look up to God in trust, rejoicing, for only in Him can you see the brighter side of life.

Or do you think that, like Daniel, you are experiencing a tough time as laws, principles, or protocols are being changed which challenge your faith as a Christian? I encourage you to remain committed to God, notwithstanding any changes. Instead, lift up holy hands in praise to God; like Daniel, He will "make Himself strong and mighty on your behalf."

AFFIRMATION

I thank you, Lord, for helping me to stay strong through all the battles and challenges of life in Jesus' name. I am strong and I know that no challenge is strong enough to defeat or kill me. I live in this consciousness. This is my reality, hallelujah! I am winning today and always, praise God.

JOURNAL

Thinking about it now, have you witnessed or experienced a time where your faith in God was tried and tested?

What did you do to strengthen your faith?

How did you keep trusting God while the situation lasted?

List two spiritual lessons that the experience taught you. What new lesson(s) have you learned today?

Day 6

DAY 7:

Praise God for Strong and Purposeful Relationships

Ephesians 5:18-20

And do not be drunk with wine, in which is dissipation; but be filled with the Spirit, speaking to one another in psalms and hymns and spiritual songs, singing and making melody in your heart to the Lord, giving thanks always for all things to God the Father in the name of our Lord Jesus Christ.

Over time, Nana had terrible experiences in relationships which made her lose her self-worth. She felt undervalued and disrespected, and so was worried about committing to any new relationships.

Like Nana, have you been hurt; do you feel let down by some of your past relationships?

Having a strong and purposeful relationship is part of everything that God has in store for you. However, you may have been hurt, or felt disappointed and let down by some of your relationships. For Jesus says in Luke 4:18, "The Spirit of the LORD is upon Me, because...He has sent Me to heal the brokenhearted...to set at liberty those who are oppressed."

God is interested in your relationships and wants to give you solid and purposeful connections that will help to build you up. However, He first presents Himself as a friend in John 15:5, "No longer do I call you servants.... but I have called you friends..."

Today, take advantage of His friendship and "enter into His gates with thanksgiving" (Psalm 100:4) and praise Him because the Word says that His plans for you are good! He says in Jeremiah 29:11, "For I know the thoughts that I think toward you, says the Lord, thoughts of peace and not of evil, to give you a future and a hope."

I would like to encourage you to memorize this scripture. It is simple, yet so powerful. If you have been hurt, or if someone just walked out of your life without a reason, be calm and trust that God is bringing great and lovely people into your life.

"What can I do to feel better?" you may ask. And you may be thinking, "My past relationships made me feel useless, small and defeated." Jude 1:20 gives us the answer that we should build ourselves up, and we do that by praying in the Holy Spirit. This may not seem like much at the beginning, but you see, you are leaning on the Holy Spirit to build you up and help you to attract the people that you need in your life, for purposeful relationships.

You have to deposit the right things into yourself in order to be confident in who you are in Christ, no matter what you go through or how you are perceived by others.

There is no painful memory from the past that God cannot heal, no darkness that cannot be eradicated, but you must yield to Him. I should let you know that these bad things or memories don't just leave you, because the enemy tries and wants to bury you deep in them. It is his way of making you stagnant, unhappy, and afraid of venturing into new, worthy relationships.

You must make up your mind today to get him out of your mind through praise! Replace the bad and painful past memories with praise. Thank God for seeing you through the trying times. Thank

Him for keeping you alive in the land of the living, knowing that the dead cannot praise God.

AFFIRMATION

Thank you God for every lesson from my past. Help me to meet and create great relationships and memories that will help me grow in You and in my life.

I am grateful for Your love towards me, and I receive newness in my mind to walk with You to build strong, lasting and purposeful relationships.

JOURNAL

List three of the most hurtful experiences that you find difficult to take out of your mind.

Choose to forgive the people in these hurtful experiences.

List three experiences that caused you to praise God.

Which of these experiences do you consider to be most beneficial to your emotional health?

Day 7

DAY 8:

Praise God for Opening Your Eyes

2 Kings 6:17

And Elisha prayed, and said, 'LORD, I pray, open his eyes that he may see.' Then the LORD opened the eyes of the young man, and he saw. And behold, the mountain was full of horses and chariots of fire all around Elisha.

Sometimes we don't take the time to appreciate where we are until we take another view. Other times, we simply believe that the view we see isn't a beautiful view or, like Elijah's servant, we only see what is physically in front of us.

Maybe this is you today. God wants you to take another view of your life, from a place of thanksgiving. He wants to open your eyes so that you can see, with the eyes of the Spirit, all the goodness He has planned for your life.

I believe that you will be amazed at what you will see.

Your life is beautiful, and colorful, but you won't see it until you take the time to look at it. Sometimes, it is not even what you want that you see. However, you can still go ahead and thank God for the journey so far, especially for His presence and love, trusting that He will take you to where you desire.

With gratitude, see yourself as a work in progress rather than as a finished product. The scripture describes us as a vessel, clay in the hand of the potter. God has not finished with you yet, so I encourage you not to shut the door or window on yourself just yet; instead, take another look at yourself, at what God has put around you or what He has put in your hands. Yes, take another look at that job, that business, that interest, that career, that hobby, profession, skill, or dream today. Be assured that you will discover things worthy of praise and thanksgiving.

Nana once lived somewhere and never really appreciated the view. In fact, she often wondered why friends would express how much they loved the view from her apartment. She'd grown accustomed to her own opinion, and it wasn't until ten years later, when it was time to move, that she looked at it differently. It took leaving for her to finally realize that it really was a spectacular view. Appreciating nature is another way of worshipping God and praising Him for His aesthetic skills!

Today, I want you to look around you again, take another look outside; there is a beautiful view out there, so do not shut the windows or the door just yet.

AFFIRMATION

Today, I am encouraged to take another look at life. I do this with thanksgiving. Though I may have crossed off or considered it too late to do some things in my life, now I am re-evaluating them. There could be a better option, and I will see what I must do to excel, and push through. I will succeed, and I praise God for the opportunity to have another view, and the strength to win in Jesus' name. Amen!

JOURNAL

What is an aspect of your life that you need to view again?

Day 8

DAY 9:

Praise God for His Righteousness

2 Corinthians 5:21

For He made Him who knew no sin to be sin for us, that we might become the righteousness of God in Him.

Psalm 7:17

I will praise the LORD according to his righteousness,
  And will sing praise to the name of the LORD Most High.

Sunam was approached at work by a colleague who told her about Jesus. She did not initially believe that the grace message was powerful enough to save or even change her. She had been a call girl and had been violated when she was young, so trusting was not one of her strengths.

She was encouraged by others who prayed for her; she believed and invited Jesus into her life. She was thankful for this gift from God.

Today, be thankful to God for sending His son, Jesus Christ to die for us and for forgiving our sins.

The Bible says that when we give our lives to God, old things are passed away and we become new and take on His nature.

God loved you so much which was why He sent His Son to die for you. Now, that was a major sacrifice! Therefore, praise Him today for this gift. Dance, for God is your salvation (Psalm 27:1) and your pathway to the life of righteousness that He wants you to live.

As you praise Him, make a commitment to live to honor Him.

One way to show God that you are grateful is to live a righteous life. Remember that a life of sin is an abomination to God. A highly moral life does not depict closeness to God, but a life of righteousness, through faith in our Lord Jesus, is what keeps you close to God.

AFFIRMATION

I believe that Jesus died for me. He was crucified and buried, but God raised Him up from the dead. Now, I live in abundance and reign in this life in righteousness through faith.

JOURNAL

How can you show God and the world that you believe you are His righteousness?

Day 9

DAY 10:

Praise God for the Vision He Has Given to You

Psalm 100:4-5

Enter into His gates with thanksgiving,
  And into His courts with praise.
  Be thankful to Him, and bless His name.

For the LORD is good;
  His mercy is everlasting,
  And His truth endures to all generations.

Hatina had plans. She wanted to make headway in her life but she didn't know the first thing about achieving goals. Then, she read a scripture in Habakkuk 2:2: "Write the vision and make it plain on tablets, that he may run who reads it." She became excited and wrote down her plan just the way she pictured it in her mind. She was full of anticipation for her next level, but a question kept nagging at her, "what if I write this down and things change, am I allowed to amend the vision?" She decided to lay it at the Lord's feet in praise and thanksgiving, trusting Him to tell her what to do about her laid out plan.

Today, like Hatina, not only should you have your vision written out, but I also want to encourage you to praise God for the wisdom and grace to write and edit the vision.

The scripture says that we should write the vision and make it plain that all who read it will run with it.

Many of us write, but then do not trust God for the fulfillment of that vision.

I would like to encourage you to write, and trust in God to direct you. When you have written the vision, God's wisdom will help you structure and work it to bring it to pass.

Do not beat yourself up because the activities change, instead, today, thank God for the ability to rewrite or update the goals and for the grace to follow them through.

As you dance today, you are stating that nothing can truly separate you from the love of God and you believe that the vision God has given to you will come to pass.

AFFIRMATION

I believe in God and in His resurrection power. I am grateful for His power in my life, the ability to envision my future and work it to fulfillment.

I put on my dancing shoes, and I celebrate for all to see that my future is assured in Christ.

JOURNAL

Where do you see yourself in the next two, three or five years?

What milestones do you see yourself accomplishing?

Take time to write down one of the goals that you want to achieve; remember to make it plain.

Praise God for the vision.

Day 10

_____
_____
_____
_____
_____
_____
_____
_____
_____
_____
_____
_____
_____
_____
_____
_____
_____
_____
_____
_____
_____
_____
_____
_____
_____
_____
_____
_____

DAY 11:

Praise God by Dancing

2 Samuel 6:14

Then David danced before the LORD with all his might; and David was wearing a linen ephod.

The scripture recounts how David danced unashamedly before the Lord. That was when He led Israel to bring the ark of the Lord into the capital city. He was glad that the presence of the Lord was being carried into the land of Israel; it was a sight to behold!

Dancing before the Lord is an act of worship. It is a sign of total submission to God for total victory in the face of trials.

Today, I want you to praise God and dance so hard that those close to you will wonder if all your problems had disappeared overnight.

Your dance is a declaration that someone more prominent is in control and is stepping into the situation with you. David ushered in God's presence with a dance; you can too!

As you dance today, you are stating that nothing can truly separate you from the love of God.

AFFIRMATION

I am dancing because I know the one whose presence I carry. I am grateful for His presence in my life.

I put on my dancing shoes and I celebrate for all to see that victory is assured in God.

JOURNAL

Dance and keep your mind on the things that make you dance unto the Almighty God.

Day 11

DAY 12:

Praise God for His Holy Spirit

Colossians 2:6-7

As you therefore have received Christ Jesus the Lord, so walk in Him, rooted and built up in Him and established in the faith, as you have been taught, abounding in it with thanksgiving.

Janet always felt alone. Her mother, a member of a particular Fellowship, took her for a meeting one day and there she learned about the Holy Spirit.

As a Christian, she was taught that we are not alone and Jesus did not abandon us, rather, before He ascended to Heaven He prayed for the Father to send us a comforter. In John 14:16, He says, "And I will pray the Father, and He will give you another Helper, that He may abide with you forever."

That night, there was an altar call for those who desired the baptism of the Holy Spirit. Janet didn't hesitate to join the line and she received the baptism of the Holy Spirit and she was prayed for.

Today, if you already have the Holy Spirit's infilling, I want you to thank God. Thank Him, for His Spirit gives life and gives you the power to win in all aspects of your life.

On this praise journey, you can receive the indwelling of the Holy Spirit if you have not yet received Him. You only have to desire His presence in your life.

In Acts 1:8, Jesus said to his disciples, "But you shall receive power when the Holy Spirit has come upon you; and you shall be witnesses to Me in Jerusalem, and in all Judea and Samaria, and to the end of the earth."

On the day of Pentecost, the Holy Spirit descended and filled the disciples. The scripture says they began to speak in new tongues in Acts 2. This is the same power that we experience today, and we have also received the ability to speak in new tongues. The Spirit gives us different gifts as He desires (1 Corinthians 12:4-11).

AFFIRMATION

Thank you, God, for the gift for the Spirit, which gives me the power to win. I receive the infilling of the Holy Spirit into my life, to help me live my life deeply rooted in God. I am blessed with various gifts by the Holy Spirit according to Your word in 1 Corinthians 12:4-11.

I praise you, Father.

JOURNAL

Read 1 Corinthians 12:4-11.

What are the gifts of the Spirit listed in this scripture passage?

Day 12

DAY 13:

Praise God for Courage

Psalm 95:1-3

Oh come, let us sing to the LORD!
Let us shout joyfully to the Rock of our salvation.

Let us come before His presence with thanksgiving;
Let us shout joyfully to Him with psalms.

For the LORD is the great God,
And the great King above all gods.

When the Philistines challenged the Israelites to a fight, David requested to challenge and fight the giant Goliath. David was Jesse's last son who was so young that he was not in the military and had only been in the field tending his father's sheep.

Before then, David was not aware of the Philistines and only found out because his father had sent him to deliver food to his brothers in the battlefield.

Upon his arrival, he requested to fight the giant, but he was rebuked by his brothers who thought that he was too inexperienced. David approached King Saul and told him of his experiences and a show of courage.

He said, "Your servant used to keep his father's sheep, and when a lion or a bear came and took a lamb out of the flock, I went out after it and struck it, and delivered the lamb from its mouth; and when it arose against me, I caught it by its beard, and struck and killed it" (1 Samuel 17:34-35).

David demonstrated courage when he volunteered to fight Goliath who was described in 1 Samuel 17:5 (TLB) as "a Philistine champion from Gath...over nine feet tall!"

Despite the fact that he was a giant who scared the whole of Israel, he did not scare a young boy who was full of courage. Courage can be seen in David's challenge to him, "For who is this uncircumcised Philistine, that he should defy the armies of the living God?" (1 Samuel 17:26).

Like David, we should have the courage in God to stand in the face of any challenge.

Today, thank the Lord for the courage to stand and fight in the face of adversity.

You have God's power in you which can be demonstrated as it was when David killed Goliath. The courage in the power of God brought him and the nation considerable success.

AFFIRMATION

Thank you, God, for the courage to stand in the face of adversity.

I trust that your Spirit helps me to always win; giving me the power to overcome any situation.

JOURNAL

What area of your life do you need to apply courage?

Day 13

_____
_____
_____
_____
_____
_____
_____
_____
_____
_____
_____
_____
_____
_____
_____
_____
_____
_____
_____
_____
_____
_____
_____
_____
_____
_____
_____
_____

DAY 14:

Praise God for His Strength to Get Up and Turn On the Lights

Psalm 9:1

I will praise You, O LORD, with my whole heart;
I will tell of all Your marvelous works.

Sophia had been in a military high school where the lights were turned off every night and you were not allowed to do anything after "lights out."

It was so strict that the military officers moved around to ensure no one was outside. Everyone had to be in bed asleep, or at least pretending to sleep.

The nightly "lights out" restricted you from reading, doing late night laundry, or anything else.

Does this sound familiar? Do you feel like it's a time of your life where the lights seem to be turned off and you cannot do much anymore? I'm not talking about a period where you are patiently anticipating something happening, but a time where you are absolutely stagnant; you seem to grope in the dark and can't see anywhere beyond where you are.

Today, God wants you to turn on your lights, and in doing this, you are allowing yourself to live and breathe again and accomplish His purpose for your life.

"How?" you might ask. You turn on the light by using the word of God.

In Psalm 119:105, the Psalmist says that, "Your word is a lamp to my feet and a light to my path."

God's word in your spirit will bring light to your whole life, and as you praise Him today, you are openly declaring with your actions that you trust in Him to help you see the next steps to take, praise God!

Remember, recanting who God says He is, what He says He will and can do, is a way of praising God. Therefore, pick up your copy of the Bible and begin to look for the scriptures where God speaks about His almightiness; say those things back to Him. Yes, praise God with His own words and turn on your lights! You can also get the music of Christian ministers to help you to turn on your lights, because they also sing about the almightiness of God and His manifold manifestations.

AFFIRMATION

I am turning on the lights in my life with the word of God. I may not look like the success I want to be or see, but today I can see with the lights on, and I will make good progress in Jesus' name. Amen.

JOURNAL

In what area of your life do you need to get up and turn on the lights? This could be in your marriage, academics, relationship, career or business.

Take stock, write them down and develop an action plan for the changes or developments you want to see.

Day 14

DAY 15:

Praise God for the Ability to Remember Your Dreams

Genesis 37:5

Joseph had a dream, and when he told it to his brothers...

Today praise God for the ability to remember the dreams that he has given you.

Joseph was born to his father Jacob at an old age and his father loved him very much. This caused his brothers to become envious of him. The envy grew more profound when he had a dream that they all perceived him as a ruler over them. Joseph was eventually sold off to strangers due to this perceived threat.

The events which unfolded in his life could have made Joseph totally forget about God or his father and his dreams, but he did not. He continued to serve God in his master's house, and God blessed him. When he was tempted by his master's wife to have sexual relations with her, he refused.

She lied to her husband and Joseph was thrown into prison for sticking to God's principles rather than committing adultery.

In prison, Joseph was admired and held on to God's promise to him. He interpreted dreams for the Pharaoh's butler and baker, who were also prisoners — these dreams revealed their futures. Joseph asked the butler to remember him but, as it is with humans, he did not remember him immediately. Not until God caused the Pharaoh to have a dream which only Joseph could interpret.

This story shows us that God will do whatever has to be done to bring to pass his promises in your life. I encourage you to read the complete story in Genesis 40 and 41, and to remain reassured. Write down your dreams, and pray about them consistently.

Like Joseph, God wants you to remember all that He has told you from His words, your dreams, visions, etc. This is because you may have allowed so many activities and situations to crowd your mind to the extent of forgetting those dreams, ambitions, visions, ideas, or even skills of greatness that God had revealed to you.

Therefore, praise Him today for using Joseph's story to make you remember your greatness that He had spoken to you, and of you! As you praise God, He will begin to speak with you about life and your purpose. I believe and pray that God will talk to you and remind you of all the things he has told you in the past.

AFFIRMATION

Thank you, Lord for blessing me and for reminding me of the words you have spoken about my life and the dreams you have shown me. Your promises are indeed yea, and amen.

I know you will complete all you have promised me, and your prophecy over my life will be established in Jesus' name. Amen.

JOURNAL

What dreams, ideas, or visions of greatness has God previously shown you?

What skills has God blessed you with? How are you using them?

Day 15

DAY 16:

Praise God for Showing Us the Power of Praise

Acts 16:25-27

But at midnight Paul and Silas were praying and singing hymns to God, and the prisoners were listening to them. Suddenly there was a great earthquake, so that the foundations of the prison were shaken; and immediately all the doors were opened and everyone's chains were loosed. And the keeper of the prison, awaking from sleep and seeing the prison doors open, supposing the prisoners had fled, drew his sword and was about to kill himself.

This story portrays the power of praise that we should always consciously activate. Yes, we ought to always praise God for His goodness in our lives; even when we are not in the most encouraging situation.

I can't say if Paul and Silas were expecting a miracle from God and so were encouraged to pray, but I know that praise was second nature to them. They couldn't just allow themselves to wallow in self-pity; they had to do what they knew was right for them to do.

You are awake today, which means that God has a plan for you, and maybe like Paul and Silas, you are experiencing a limitation or a delay. You can pray and praise God ahead of the victory coming your way! I believe that God will hear you.

David never lost any battle because he never went into any without first consulting God; he understood the source of his strength and victory.

The Psalms are filled with his praise to God, even in dire times. Praise God and encourage others around you to do the same.

AFFIRMATION

Dear Father, I praise you with my whole heart. "From the rising of the sun to its going down the LORD's name is to be praised" (Psalm 113:3).

JOURNAL

Are you experiencing a difficult challenge like Paul and Silas?

What things will you do differently now that you are studying about praise?

Read and reflect on Psalm 100.

Day 16

DAY 17:

Praise God for Your Identity in Christ

2 Corinthians 5:17

Therefore, if anyone is in Christ, he is a new creation; old things have passed away; behold, all things have become new.

Today, I would like you to reflect on your identity in Christ and thank God for who He has made you to be.

You must be thankful to God for the ability to reflect on this, for to be thoughtful about the workings of God is to be thankful.

We are not small or insignificant in his eyes. We are the apple of his eye, and he loves us unconditionally.

AFFIRMATION

I declare today that I belong to Jesus Christ.
I live by the word of God.
I receive the comfort and guidance of the Holy Spirit.
I am an overcomer in Jesus' Name.

JOURNAL

There are so many things God has said about you in the bible. Take time to search them out and write them down, starting with "I am..." For example:

> I am a bright and shining light.
> I am the righteousness of God in Christ Jesus.
> I am the healed of God.
> I am a Champion and fear has no grip on me.

Don't just write these claims, learn to confess them at all times.

Praise God, and make Him proud with your identity!

Day 17

DAY 18:

Praise God for a Renewed Mind

Romans 12:1-2

I beseech you therefore, brethren, by the mercies of God, that you present your bodies a living sacrifice, holy, acceptable to God, which is your reasonable service. And do not be conformed to this world, but be transformed by the renewing of your mind, that you may prove what is that good and acceptable and perfect will of God.

Though we have learned that we are new creatures when we come to accept Jesus as our Lord, because we believe in His finished work of redemption, we have the responsibility of renewing our minds. This we must do, if we actually want to experience the change that has been worked out for us. The scripture says that we have the mind of Christ. "...But we have the mind of Christ" (1 Corinthians 2:16).

The first step to receiving a renewed mind, is to receive Jesus as your Lord and Savior. You become born again and your experience with the Lord begins. One benefit of being a Christian is that you receive a renewed mind. So today you will praise God for giving you a renewed mind.

AFFIRMATION

Jesus was crucified that I may live and not die; therefore, I live in this life with a renewed mindset. I have God's nature of righteousness in me. I have a renewed mind in Christ. Hallelujah!

JOURNAL

Search the scriptures to study more about a renewed mind in Christ.

Itemize some of the scriptures you have found, and the lessons learned. Here is one to start off with:
1 Corinthians 2:16 "For 'who has known the mind of the LORD that he may instruct Him?' But we have the mind of Christ."

Day 18

DAY 19:

Praise God for the Grace to Hear

Sarah heard what the angel said to her husband Abraham in Genesis 18:10 (NIV), "I will surely return to you about this time next year, and Sarah your wife will have a son."

She laughed and thought, "After I am worn out, and my lord is old, will I now have this pleasure?" (Genesis 18:12, NIV).

Although Sarah laughed because she observed her physical condition, she was granted the grace to hear the prophecy.

It is a great gift to be able to hear what God is saying to you. The Bible says in Deuteronomy 29:29, "The secret things belong to the LORD our God, but those things which are revealed belong to us."

Today, I want you to praise God for His ability to speak to you as well as for the privilege of hearing Him.

In 1 Samuel 3, we read about how Samuel was lying down in the house of the Lord, where the ark of God was. Then, he heard someone call out his name. Though he answered, he didn't know it was God calling out to him until Eli told him and advised him on how to respond to the voice, if he heard it again. This was the beginning of Samuel's walk with God. Notice that he was in God's presence, as the ark expressly symbolizes God's presence. Samuel was graced to hear God's voice.

Today thank God for the grace to hear and know that He is the one calling out and speaking to you. Rejoice for you are blessed and remembered by the Lord today!

AFFIRMATION

Dear Father, thank you for the grace to hear from you and to obey your voice in Jesus' name. Reveal yourself more to me, by your Holy Spirit.

JOURNAL

What does the scripture say about hearing from God?

What has God been telling you about your situation?

Day 19

DAY 20:

Praise God for the Ability to Believe His Word

Jeremiah 32:27

Behold, I am the LORD, the God of all flesh. Is anything too hard for Me?

Winnie and the love of her life, Harry, had been believing that God would bless them with a child for a long time now.

Both had been through several hospital tests and still there was no sign of a baby, but they decided to trust in God.

They searched the scriptures and kept trusting God daily. One of the scriptures they confessed was a boast that God made of Himself; a rhetorical question that He asked in our open verse today. They never stopped to ask themselves, "Is there anything too hard for God to do?" They believed and boasted of the God that is not careful to boast that He can do all things!

This is enough reason to praise God, and dance before Him! Today, are you ready to praise and thank God for whom you believe He is?

I pray that we have the grace to believe God that He is who He says that He is.

I would like you to meditate on the scripture in Jeremiah 32:27 and praise God for His love, wherein He has loved us. Counting it as a joy when you go through every challenge (James 1:2).

AFFIRMATION

I will look out for good things, even in uncomfortable places. I will always see positive things in every situation that I find myself. I trust in God to take care of me.

I believe His word always, no matter what I am going through. My testimony and victory are on the way, praise God!

JOURNAL

What are the big things that you believe in God for?

Study James 1:2.

Find 5 scriptures on faith that you will stand on for your miracle(s).

Day 20

DAY 21:

Praise God, for Your Portion Is Blessed

As God's child, there is an allotted plot for you; praise God, for your portion is large!

Today's content is slightly different; I would like you to read out the scripture below and meditate on the words with gratitude in your heart that your portion is blessed.

Wherever you find yourself, you must remember that you are blessed.

Oko had always felt that his rich father had passed away without really leaving them much. He had recently been studying the scriptures because his friend had introduced him to God and had been taking him to Church.

Every time he was asked "How are you?" he simply said, "I am blessed." Studying the Word had helped him to realize that he could rely on God's portion for him, which the Bible describes as large. He dedicated time to studying God's plans and blessings for him and started to live and walk in this consciousness and speak the Word over his life.

Yes, his portion was large and blessed! Like Oko, today learn to speak God's word over your life. You are blessed and your portion is large.

Study the scripture below and say it over and over until the words stick within your spirit.

Deuteronomy 28:3-14

Blessed shall you be in the city, and blessed shall you be in the country.

Blessed shall be the fruit of your body, the produce of your ground and the increase of your herds, the increase of your cattle and the offspring of your flocks.

Blessed shall be your basket and your kneading bowl.

Blessed shall you be when you come in, and blessed shall you be when you go out.

The LORD will cause your enemies who rise against you to be defeated before your face; they shall come out against you one way and flee before you seven ways.

The LORD will command the blessing on you in your storehouses and in all to which you set your hand, and He will bless you in the land which the LORD your God is giving you.

The LORD will establish you as a holy people to Himself, just as He has sworn to you, if you keep the commandments of the LORD your God and walk in His ways. Then all peoples of the earth shall see that you are called by the name of the LORD, and they shall be afraid of you. And the LORD will grant you plenty of goods, in the fruit of your body, in the increase of your livestock, and in the produce of your ground, in the land of which the LORD swore to your fathers to give you. The LORD will open to you His good treasure, the heavens, to give the rain to your land in its season, and to bless all the work of your hand. You shall lend to many nations, but you shall not borrow. And the LORD will make you the head and not the tail; you shall be above only, and not be beneath, if you heed the commandments of the LORD your God, which I command you today, and are careful to observe them. So you shall not turn aside from any of the words which I command you this day, to the right or the left, to go after other gods to serve them.

AFFIRMATION

I am blessed; everywhere I go, I am blessed.
In my going out and coming in, I am blessed.

JOURNAL

Write down more affirmations for your large portion.

Day 21

DAY 22:

Praise God for the Gift of Prayer & Communion

Matthew 26:26-28

And as they were eating, Jesus took bread, blessed and broke it, and gave it to the disciples and said, "Take, eat; this is My body."

Then he took the cup, and gave thanks, and gave it to them, saying, "Drink from it, all of you. For this is My blood of the new covenant, which is shed for many for the remission of sins.

Today, praise God for the gift of the communion and for teaching us how to communicate with Him. There is so much power in the communion and in prayer, so today thank God for giving us this revelation.

God desires a sincere relationship with you, and He always hears you and your heartfelt, continuous prayer avails much (James 5:16).

Jesus, before His crucifixion, observed the Jewish Passover feast with His disciples. However, this was no ordinary feast as, for the first time, Jesus instituted what we presently call the communion (the bread and wine symbolising His flesh and blood). Jesus also encouraged them to always do this.

Similarly, we also should take the communion to remember His death and the price He paid for us.

AFFIRMATION

I am thankful to you God, for the gift of prayer and communion.

Daily, I use prayer and communion to grow my relationship with God and win in my life affairs. Thank you, Jesus.

JOURNAL

When last did you have the communion?

What are your personal convictions or experiences about it?

Day 22

DAY 23:

Praise God, for You Have Been Set Up for Victory

1 John 5:4:

For whatever is born of God overcomes the world. And this is the victory that has overcome the world—our faith.

We are victorious through Jesus Christ our Lord and, as each day comes with challenges, we have grace to win every day.

As God's child, you are set up for victory. Jeremiah 1:5 says that before you were formed in your mother's womb, God knew you, so be assured that He has your entire life planned ahead of time.

The Lord will cause the enemies who rise up against you to be defeated before you. They will come at you from one direction but flee from you in seven (Deuteronomy 28:7).

You must realize that nothing is significant enough to withstand you. Isaiah 59:19 says that, "So shall they fear the name of the LORD from the west, and His glory from the rising of the sun; when the enemy comes in like a flood, the Spirit of the LORD will lift up a standard against him."

The scripture says that the enemy will come in, but the Lord is for you and will lift up a standard against him.

I wonder what is making you worried or fearful today? Let these words be in you that your enemies have been smitten; you cannot be defeated, and you will not fail. And yes, you can begin to praise God in the knowledge of your already won battles, struggles and challenges! Praise and dance your way to victory!

AFFIRMATION

Dear Father, today I am reminded that I have been set up for victory. I am grateful that You count me worthy of success.

Lord, I praise You for equipping me for success.

Thank you, Lord, for the strength to win.

JOURNAL

Write down the victories God has given to you.

Day 23

DAY 24:

Praise God for the Ability to Wait

Philippians 4:6-7

Be anxious for nothing, but in everything by prayer and supplication, with thanksgiving, let your requests be made known unto God and the peace of God, which surpasses all understanding will guard your hearts and minds through Christ Jesus.

Waiting is not always comfortable or pleasant, and the Word says that we should "be anxious for nothing."

Is there anything troubling you today, or making you anxious? Your response should be, "I refuse to be anxious for nothing."

How you wait is described in Ephesians 6:13-17: "Therefore take up the whole armor of God, that you may be able to withstand in the evil day, and having done all, to stand.

Stand therefore, having girded your waist with truth, having put on the breastplate of righteousness, and having shod your feet with the preparation of the gospel of peace, above all, taking the shield of faith with which you will be able to quench all the fiery darts of the wicked one. And take the helmet of salvation, and the sword of the Spirit, which is the word of God."

This should excite you!

Waiting in Christianity doesn't mean remaining stagnant. It means believing in God to make true His promises. It is being joyful and grateful, praising God and doing what the Word says while trusting His promises to come to pass.

The Scripture shows us various people of faith who exhibited strength while waiting on the Lord. Romans 4:3 says, "Abraham believed God, and it was accounted to him for righteousness." So, let's learn to wait and to believe God.

Read Isaiah 40:31 and get excited in your spirit. Praise God for the ability to wait!

AFFIRMATION

I am strong, bold and patient. I am a believing child of God and winning even while I wait. I can see with the eyes of the Spirit that my victory is here.

JOURNAL

Study more about patience and record what you learn.

Day 24

DAY 25:

Praise God for the Holy Spirit & for His Power

Acts 1:8

But you shall receive power when the Holy Spirit has come upon you: and you shall be witnesses to Me in Jerusalem, and in all Judea and Samaria, and to the end of the earth.

After the resurrection, Jesus instructed the disciples to wait in Jerusalem because God the Father would send the Holy Spirit to be with them and to empower them for the life ahead.

Today, praise God for sending the Holy Spirit. By the Holy Spirit, we have received God's dynamic power to win every day.

The Scripture tells us about the gifts of the spirits. Live in this consciousness that God's Spirit is at work in you.

If you haven't received the Holy Spirit and you are wondering how you can, ask the Lord to baptize you with His Spirit. Luke 11:13 says, "If you then, being evil, know how to give good gifts to your children, how much more will your heavenly Father give the Holy Spirit to those who ask him!"

AFFIRMATION

I am not alone; I have the Holy Spirit to lead and help me. He directs me in all my affairs and allows me to win consistently.

JOURNAL

Do you remember the day you got saved, how did you feel? What was your experience?

Have you been baptized by the Holy Spirit? How did you feel? What was your experience?

If you haven't been baptized by the Holy Spirit, don't forget to write about your experience when He does.

Day 25

DAY 26:

Praise God, for His Yoke Is Easy and Burden Light

Matthew 11:28-30

Come to Me, all you who labor and are heavy laden, and I will give you rest. Take My yoke upon you and learn from Me, for I am gentle and lowly in heart, and you will find rest for your souls. For My yoke is easy and My burden is light.

Before mechanized farming began, animals like cows, donkeys, or horses were yoked in pairs and used to plow the field for a planting season. The farmer ensured that the two animals were of equal strength so that they could work in unison. If one became weak, the stronger one would pull it by the yoke. Inherently, Jesus says He is the stronger one and urges us to take up His yoke and burden. We do not have to bear any burden or work as hard, because He has done all the hard work!

Again, this should excite you to rise up and praise God!!!

Rejoice in the Lord if you have followed Him but feel weighed down. The good news for you is that Jesus said in Matthew 16:24-26, "If anyone desires to come after Me, let him deny himself, and take up his cross, and follow Me. For whoever desires to save his life will lose it, but whoever loses his life for My sake will find it. For what profit is it to a man if he gains the whole world, and loses his own soul? Or what will a man give in exchange for his soul?"

Be assured today that as you walk with the Lord daily, you will definitely find your life's purpose and His blessings will remain visible in your life.

Since we are on a praise journey, I want to remind you that praise is one of the ways we can walk with God. I'm not talking about paying lip service, but to sincerely acknowledge God in all your ways and praise Him for your redemption.

In 1 Peter 5:7, the Word says that you should give all of your worries and cares to God, for He cares about you. Today, as you praise Him, surrender all your fears and take to Him, and take on His yoke.

AFFIRMATION

As I take up the cross to follow Jesus, I am convinced that my life is complete and full of grace and great accomplishments.

I am blessed and highly favored.

JOURNAL

What are the cares you want to cast on the Lord?

Day 26

DAY 27:

Praise God for His Wisdom

James 1:5

If any of you lacks wisdom, let him ask of God, who gives to all liberally and without reproach, and it will be given to him.

Susan needed God's wisdom for a major decision in her life. She had received an email that had the potential to change the direction of her life plans.

Naturally, she was very organized and thoughtful in weighing the advantages and disadvantages of her options.

Susan couldn't decide and had no idea what the consequences of her choice would be.

Her friend, Shanelle, advised her to take it one day at a time and to pray to God. She was running out of time. The two options both seemed that they would lead to acceptable outcomes, but only God could really tell her which way to go.

Susan decided to listen to Shanelle's advice and she prayed to God for wisdom and guidance.

God heard her and helped her to make the right decision.

What a privilege to know that we can ask God for His wisdom, and receive it.

In 2 Chronicles 1:10 Solomon asked God for wisdom, and God gave him wisdom and riches! Isn't God awesome?! He gives us what we ask for, and even more; as Nigerians will say, "*jara.*"

If you have been making wrong decisions, it is time to correct your decision-making style by asking God for wisdom. You can make huge successful strides in life with God's wisdom, just like Joseph, Esther, Ruth, Daniel, etc.

Today, praise God and ask Him for His wisdom, and I believe that He will hear you.

AFFIRMATION

God, thank you for giving me your wisdom to utilize in all the affairs of my life.

JOURNAL

What do you need God's wisdom for in your life today?

Day 27

DAY 28:

Praise God for Your Healing

Isaiah 53:5

But He was wounded for our transgressions,
He was bruised for our iniquities;
The chastisement for our peace was upon Him,
And by His stripes we are healed.

Praise and glory to the one true God who sent His Son to give His life for us.

The scripture above refers to Jesus and it says that Jesus took responsibility for our sins, wickedness, and transgressions. He took all the beating and torture meant for us; and the wounds that bled Him are our tickets for healing.

Healing is God's unique gift to us, and today I want us to thank God for His healing.

The scriptures record various healing miracles, and this is the joy that we have, that the same power is available for us today.

Are you in need of healing for yourself or a loved one? We are enjoined to come boldly to God's presence, but not without praise. "Let us therefore come boldly to the throne of grace, that we may obtain mercy and find grace to help in time of need" (Hebrews 4:16).

AFFIRMATION

I am the healed of God. Every sickness or symptom in my body dies from the root in Jesus' name.

God is my healer, and I trust that His blood that was shed on the cross is working on my behalf today.

The enemy is defeated, and his power of sin and sickness is broken.

Thank you, Jesus.

JOURNAL

What are you trusting God to heal in your life?

Write down healing scriptures that you will meditate on daily as you trust God for your healing.

Day 28

DAY 29:

Praise God for Your Family

Welcome to Day 29!

Today, praise God for your family. The family you were born into, the family you have created, and for friends that you can call family.

God loves families and that was why it was the first thing that He instituted after creation. God intentionally put us in families, so we can enjoy communal life with people of the same bloodline.

In Genesis 7, God saved Noah and his family. He said to Noah, "Go into the ark, you and your whole family, because I have found you righteous in this generation." (Genesis 7:1, NIV). There are so many other events in the Bible where we can see that when God saves a man, He usually saves him and his family. I believe that God's desire is for you and your family to be saved.

Thank Him for your family, and for their individual lives. Pray specifically for them individually, and thank God for helping them through the challenges of life that they may face.

God wants you closer to your family and to consistently spend time praying for them.

AFFIRMATION

Thank you, Lord, for my family. I am grateful that I have one and I love them.

Keep us strong and full of strength to serve you all the days of our lives in Jesus' name. Amen.

"As for me and my house, we will serve the LORD!" (Joshua 24:15).

JOURNAL

Which of your family members do you need to specifically pray for their salvation?

Which member of your family have you not reached out to for a while?

Why haven't you reached out to that person?

Think about what you love most about this person and write a tribute to the person via SMS, postcard, or any of the social media platforms.

I encourage you to do this often for every member of your family; not just on their birthdays or wedding anniversaries.

Day 29

DAY 30:

Praise God for the Progress You Are Making

Congratulations on completing this devotion.

Today we will specifically thank God for His various blessings and grace in different areas of our life.

Go over the 30 topics and the notes you made in your journal and praise God for the grace to complete it.

Praise Him for helping you serve Him.

Praise Him for helping you grow in your relationship with Him.

Praise Him for helping you succeed in life.

AFFIRMATION

I will not stop praising God;

I will not get too busy to stay in His presence.

I will never honor my problems above God.

I will praise God every day of my life!

JOURNAL

Write five things that you have learned from this journey.

Day 30

NEXT STEPS

The sound of a healthy baby being born is the sound of cries.

This brings joy to all who are witnesses to the birth of the baby. Usually, crying signifies sadness, but this is a time when it means happiness.

Today, the picture God shows is that as you praise Him, you will experience the sort of joy that is only experienced in a room when a baby is born, where both baby and mother are doing well.

You have waited long enough for this baby, and now you are birthing your dream. Your anticipated change is here!

AFFIRMATION

I am blessed; everywhere I go, I am blessed.
In my going out and coming in, I am blessed.

JOURNAL

How do you plan to continue on this journey?

Draw out a workable plan and be intentional about it.

Notes

Notes

Notes

Printed in the United States
by Baker & Taylor Publisher Services